CHAKRA STONES

The Beginner's Guide to the Healing Power of Crystals and the Complete Balance of Your Chakras

Jay K. Morley

Sibiu, 2021

ISBN 978-973-0-35436-2

Table of Contents

Introduction

The absolute best thing you could do to keep your energetic system in check is to perform a regular chakra tune-up. As our dynamic 'organs,' the chakras work alongside our physical, emotional, and mental. These chakras both influence and are influenced by our daily activities and even our nutrition.

We cannot shut our chakras off, just like we can't shut off our organs, and just like our physical organs, our chakras too can get fatigued and depleted over time. If we are exposed to too many low frequencies, such as traumatic events, lack of self-care, and reduced stress management, our chakras can also be blocked. It causes all kinds of different symptoms, such as physical pain and feelings of depression, to name a few.

Thankfully, there are numerous different ways through which you can cleanse and revitalize your chakras. One of the easiest ways to do this is through crystals. Crystals affect our chakras by lifting their vibration, clearing them, and spinning at an optimal rate.

Crystals possess higher vibrational frequencies, and just being around them and setting your intention to attune to their vibration can profoundly affect your overall health. Additionally, each crystal has its exclusive energetic properties and can thus be used strategically to enhance lethargy and subdue overactivity in the chakras.

Through this book, I aim to highlight how you can use crystals to heal your chakras. Remember that you can get as fancy when it comes to crystal healing as you like; however, do not confuse fanciness with effectiveness.

A Brief History of the Chakras

Before you begin any journey, it is essential to know where you are starting. Learning to recognize all the different chakras within yourself and all others will help you transform how you spend your life in this world. However, to understand, heal, and balance the chakras, it is imperative to know what you are studying precisely. So let us first start with a brief history of the chakra system.

The Vedas, written from 2000 to 600 B.C., depicts the Aryans invading India on chariots. The original word 'cakra' or 'chakra' is written in the text. The meaning of chakras is a wheel, and it refers to the wheels of the chariots that this group of individuals used. This wheel is crucial as it represents the eternal and cyclical nature of time.

The sun, whose path is also cyclical, is the center of balance for our planet. In this manner, the wheel, or chakras, is symbolic of celestial order and stability in our personal lives. Chakras are again mentioned in the Yoga Upanishads (circa 600 A.D), and in the Yoga Sutras of Patanjali (circa 200 B.C). In the 10th century, a text Gorakshashatakam was written, which explains numerous meditation techniques related to the chakras.

The primary texts explaining the chakras were the Sat-Cakra-Nirupana, written in 1577, along with the Padaka-Pancaka of the

10th century. Both of these texts describe the seven chakra centers and practices related to maintaining and restoring balance. Arthur Avalon also translated these texts into English in 1919 in his book "The Serpent Power." It is through this book that the Western World was introduced to the idea of chakras.

Chakra Basics

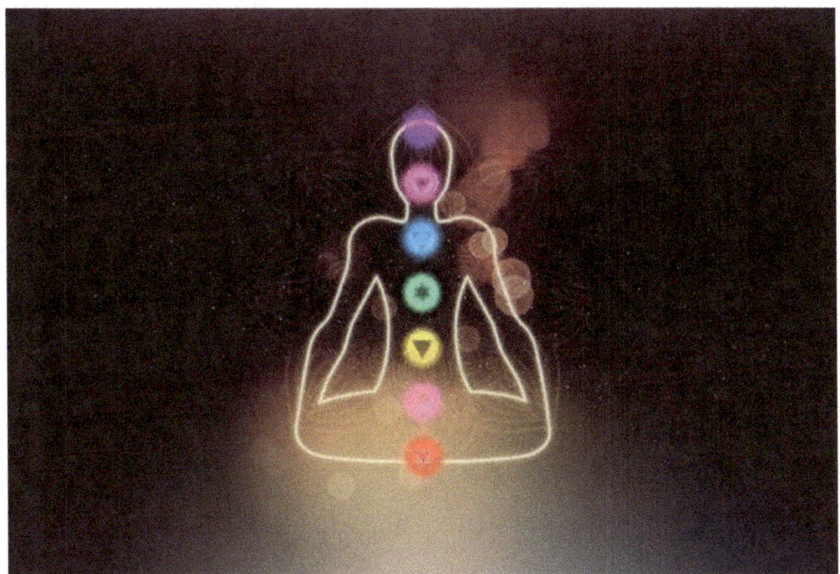

At the core of this system are seven chakras, which serve as the body's basic energy centers. The seven chakras correspond to all the seven major nerve ganglia of the body, which branch out from the spinal cord. The fact that all the ancient texts perfectly described the nerve centers well before western medicine added a level of credibility to the system of chakras and related sister sciences.

The six lower chakras, except the crown, have three major energy channels that run through them, known as Nadis. Susumna is one of the most efficient for carrying energy as it runs up and down the spine. The Ida Nadi crisscrosses through the chakras and passes them through the left nostril.

The Pingala Nadi also weaves a pattern through the chakras, which passes through the right nostril. In a healthy and balanced being, energy flows uninhibited through the chakras. Nonetheless, most people have chakras blocked by impurity or another, which forces the flow of energy solely through Ida and Pingala, and completely avoids the "energy highway" Susumna.

Both the external situations and the internal habits, for instance, the tension that usually disturbs the body or leads to negative thoughts about oneself, can lead to a chakra to become imbalanced. When the chakras are not balanced correctly, your body does not work as efficiently as possible, forcing some chakras to overcompensate while others are forced into submission. When this occurs, your body pays the price, physically, emotionally, as well as spiritually.

Furthermore, chakras are affected by numerous problems we deal with in life and how we choose to deal with them internally and externally in our communications with the world. As centers of force, it helps think about the chakras as physical locations where we receive, absorb, and distribute all our life energies.

Each one of the seven chakras correlates to a specific function within the body, which starts from the root at the base of the spine and work their way up through the genitals, navel, throat, center of the forehead, and the crown of the head. Once a chakra is no longer functional, the results appear in various manners, which are apparent to the eye.

The chakras rely heavily on each other to function properly. It is just impossible to find the right balance even if one chakra is overlooked. The ultimate goal is to bring the balance, which is known as Sattva, to all the chakras through a blend of activity and passivity, which leads to harmony and balance in your life. When this balance takes place, not only will your body function correctly, but your mind and spirit will also be freed, which allows you to live in a state of profound gratitude and joy. The beauty of this entire process is that it affects not only your life but also the lives of all those who are around you.

Understanding the Seven Chakras

1st Chakra: Muladhara: "Root Center"

Muladhara chakra, or the root center, is the foundation that supports our physical life. Therefore, it is essential to keep it strong and stable. This chakra helps our physical body and all the different energies and consciousness that need a body to unfold.

This chakra is situated at the root of our vertical axis, the spine, and is associated with the four basic instincts food, sleep, sex, and self-preservation.

1. Location: Base of spine
2. Function: Keeping you grounded and efficient, desire to procreate, and want of material security; creating loyalty

3. Element: Earth

4. Color: Red

5. Mantra: "I Am Here"

2nd Chakra: Svadhishthana: "Abode Of the Self" or "Identity Chakra"

The svadhisthana chakra is connected with water. This energy center offers uninterrupted access to flow, flexibility, plus fun. While working with this chakra, you are going to address your relationship with both others as well as yourself.

1. Location: Basin of the pelvis around the genital area and below the navel

2. Function: Source of our sexuality, desires, lusts, and greed. Drives our creativity, sense of self, and relationships with others.

3. Element: Water

4. Color: Orange

5. Mantra: "I Want"

3rd Chakra: Manipura: "Gem Center"

The third chakra, which is known as Manipura, translates as "lustrous gem." This is the real Sanskrit name for the Solar Plexus chakra. It is situated around the navel in the solar plexus area and up to the breastbone; it is also a source of personal power and governs self-esteem, warrior energy, and the ultimate power of transformation. The Manipura chakra moreover also controls metabolism and digestion.

1. Location: Navel, specifically around the solar plexus, and the digestive system

2. Function: Source of the emotions, feelings, intuitions, harmony, as well as transformation. Determines whether a person feels introverted or extroverted, self-confident or unconfident.

3. Element: Fire

4. Color: Yellow

5. Mantra: "I Can"

4th Chakra: Anahata: "Un-Struck" or "Unhurt", Heart Center

The primary purpose of the heart chakra is connection through feeling. Through the heart chakra we truly feel the link to our soul and the greater meaning of life. As individuals, we feel like part of a bigger unity of all life and realize that all is interconnected within a complicated web of relationships.

1. Location: Heart

2. Function: Source of compassion and unconditional love translating into one's ability to share and serve selflessly.

3. Element: Air

4. Color: Green

5. Mantra: "I Give And Receive Love"

5th Chakra: Vishuddha: "Control Center" or "Purification"

The Throat chakra is the fifth chakra. This chakra is situated at the center of the neck at the throat level and is the passageway of the energy between the lower body parts and the head. The purpose of the Throat chakra is entirely driven by the principle of expression as well as communication.

1. Location: Neck, throat, jaw, and mouth

2. Function: Creation of separate voice and communiqué, as well as ability to listen to others, helps one to accept compliments as well as criticism with ease.

3. Element: Sound or Ether (clear sky beyond clouds)

4. Color: Blue

5. Mantra: "I Speak"

6th Chakra: Ajna: "Third Eye" or "Command Center"

The gift of this chakra sees both the inner as well as the outer worlds. The energy of this chakra helps us experience clear thoughts and gifts of spiritual contemplation and self-reflection. Through this gift of seeing, we can successfully internalize the outer world, and through symbolic language, we can externalize the inner world.

1. Location: Between and slightly above the eyes; the center of the brain

2. Function: Self-realization and intuition, seeing the "big picture" as well as beyond the physical (clairvoyance, telepathy, intuition, dreaming, imagination, visualization)

3. Element: Light or Bliss (Mahat)

4. Color: Indigo

5. Mantra: "I See"

7th Chakra: Sahasrara: "Unbound" or "Infinite", the Seat Of The Soul

The seventh chakra is the crown chakra. This chakra is positioned at the top of the head; it gives us access to higher cognizance states as we open to what is beyond our fixations and visions. The function of this chakra is motivated by consciousness and helps us get in touch with the universal.

1. Location: Crown of the head
2. Function: Realization of the infinite, spirit, Divine God, universe, and unity; enlightenment and spiritual connection; ability to receive understanding and knowledge
3. Element: Universal intelligence (Satchitdananda) of Thought/Meditation
4. Color: White (sometimes depicted as Violet)
5. Mantra: Silence

RIGHTS OF 7 CHAKRAS

 TO KNOW

 TO SEE

 TO SPEAK

 TO LOVE

 TO ACT

 TO FEED

 TO BE HERE

Recognizing Imbalances in the Chakras

When a chakra is not properly functioning, it can lead to a ripple effect throughout our lives and those around us. At any given moment, depending upon a huge range of circumstances, both positive as well as negative, the energy in the chakra can get stuck or excessive, which can lead to an imbalance in the system.

Those who are in tune with their system will be able to recognize these changes and begin working towards correcting themselves. These corrections can be done through simple exercises, some life changes, yoga, and meditation, to name a few.

Often, the energy in a chakra is stuck only for a matter of minutes, while at other times, it can be stagnant for years, and sometimes even a lifetime. You can use the following reference guide to recognize the imbalances in the seven chakras. Through this chapter, I aim to show how a weakness, whether in deficiency or excess, in a specific chakra can manifest negatively in your day to day activities.

1st: Muladhara (Root Chakra)

1. Feeling of being overcome by personal life, work, and responsibilities that result in either extreme stress or just completely giving up

2. Stressed due to a "survival crises" health, money, home, and family

3. Piles of mess, "to-do" lists, and chores that don't get moved or accomplished

4. Often termed as a messy and confused person

5. Travel frequently

6. Resilient to exercise, healthy diet, as well as fresh air

7. Gluttony, hoarding money or assets

8. A profound sense of often feeling ungrounded. Living inside the head instead of the body

2nd: Svadhishthana (Pelvic Chakra)

1. Prefer solitude due to fear of judgment

2. Feelings of uncertainty or not being safe

3. Feeling "stuck" in your professional or personal relation-
    ships, or both

4. A strong desire of wanting somebody to take good care of
    you

5. Neediness

6. Self-described "overachievers"

7. Growing up in a situation where emotions were repressed
    or completely denied

8. History of sexual abuse and issues when it comes to ex-
    pressing alongside experiencing sexuality

9. Chronic pain in the lower back and hips

10. Reproductive health problems

11. A strong yearning to exhibit power over others to create an extremely false sense of confidence

12. A personality subjugated by either shyness or aggressiveness

3rd: Manipura (Navel Chakra)

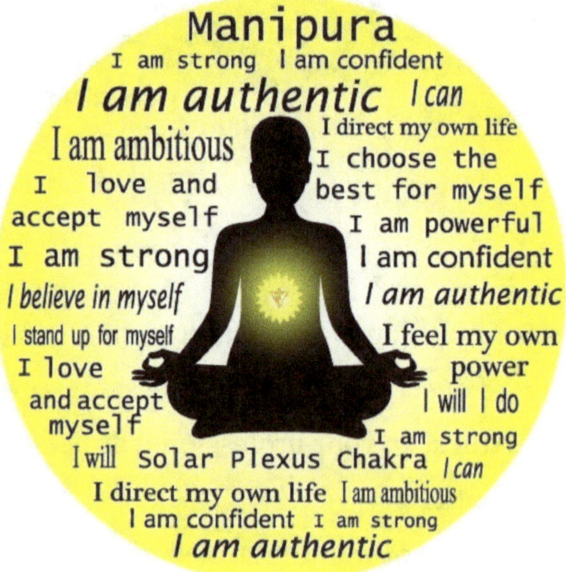

1. A profound feeling that life is puzzling, unsatisfying, and scary

2. Making decisions based upon pure emotion and/or selfishness

3. Habitual bouts of anger, sadness, along with intense emotional pain

4. History of gastric problems and/or eating disorders

5. Extremely low self-esteem

6. Sensitive to a number of stimuli which results in coping mechanisms for instance drugs, alcohol, overeating, and other types of self-abuse

7. A desire to be a perfectionist

8. A compulsive need of self-protection or protection of others

4th: Anahata (Heart Chakra)

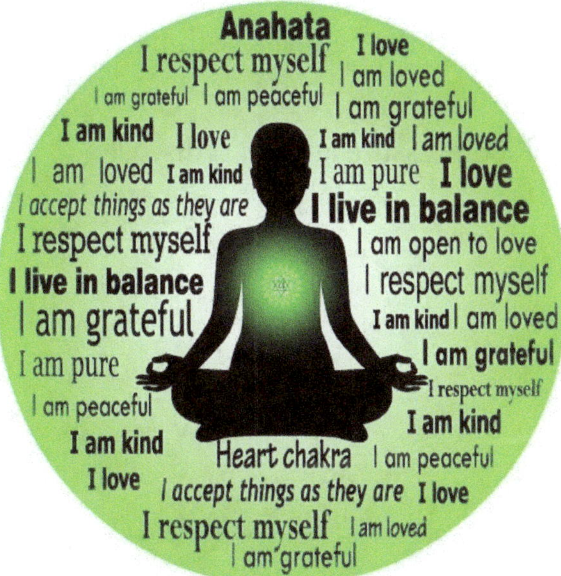

1. Regular negative emotional responses to painful or problematic life experiences

2. A life driven by fear or misconception

3. Apprehensions and emotional scars that are dealt with on a consistent basis

4. Failing to forgive or let go

5. Lack of compassion

6. A strong connection to the result of an experience rather than thankfulness for an experience

7. Fear of letting people get too close into your personal world

8. Intense shyness or loneliness

9. Struggle to receive or give love fully

10. Deep misery, selfishness, insignificance, and even hate

11. Shallow breathing patterns, asthma, along with lung diseases

12. High blood pressure and heart disease

5th: Vishuddha (Throat Chakra)

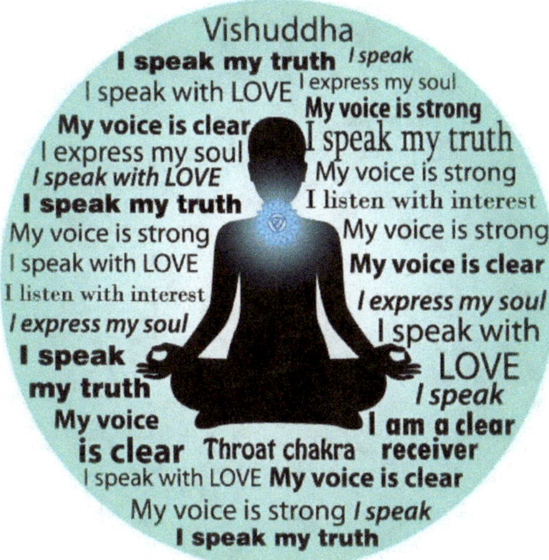

1. A feeling of being insufficient, fearful of making mistakes

2. Abuse of power or lack of power

3. Often surrounded by destructive people

4. A fondness for gossip or habitually speaking without thinking

5. Particularly shy, specifically when it comes to speaking in front of a group of people

6. Struggle with accepting compliments

7. Trouble listening to others

8. Smokers or tobacco users

9. Victims of recurrent allergies

10. Repeated sore throats and/or thyroid problems

11. Stiff necks as well as shoulders, teeth grinding, and jaw disorders

6th: Ajna (Third Eye Chakra)

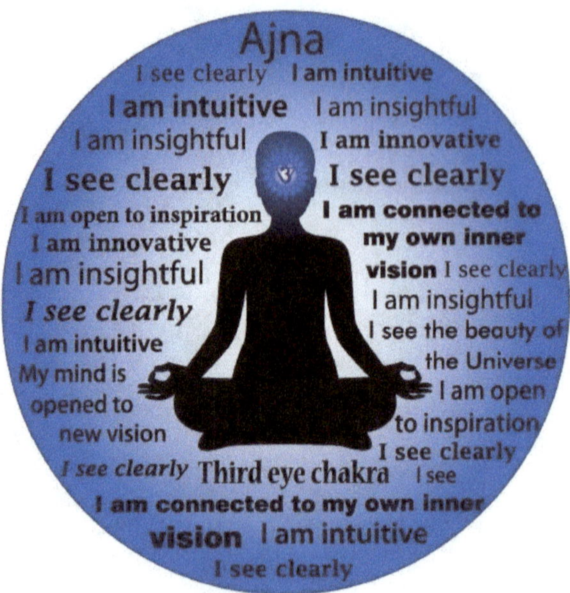

1. Follow trends as well as people blindly, unaware to possibly dangerous situations

2. Lack of ingenuity

3. Incompetence to focus or concentrate during day to day tasks

4. Find it problematic to make decisions as the situation does not seem clear

5. Oversensitive to the feelings and behavior of the people around them

6. Frequent headaches, hallucinations, and nightmares

7. Poor memory and/or eye problem

7th: Sahasrara (Crown Chakra)

1. An incapability to still the mind

2. A terror to do something today due to a traumatic past experience

3. Acting without the use of innate intuition

4. Apathetic

5. An inability to think for yourself

6. A spiritual skeptic

7. Frequent avaricious urges and shopping addictions

8. Overreaction to ignorance, both yours and others

9. An incompetence to think essentially, almost always resorting on analytical knowledge that is learned from schools as well as institutions

10. Viewing yourself as an elite member of a spiriteable

ROOT
Muladhara

"I AM SAFE. ALL FRAGMENTS OF ME ARE SAFE. I RECOGNIZE ALL FRAGMENTS OF HIGHER-SELF WITHOUT SACRIFICING MY SAFETY."

SACRAL

Sradhisthana

"I AM FREE. I AM FREE OF JUDGEMENT. I AM
FREE TO MOVE, FEEL AND BE EXACTLY WHO
I CHOOSE TO BE. I AM FREE TO CREATE AND
ACCEPT ABUNDANCE IN MY LIFE."

SOLAR PLEXUS

Manipura

"I AM IN CHARGE. I AM THE DIVINE CREATOR OF
MY REALITY. I TAKE FULL ACCOUNTABILITY AND
RESPONSIBILITY FOR MY CHOICES, BEHAVIOR AND
ACTIONS THAT UNHEALED VERSIONS OF ME MADE.
I UNDERSTAND ONLY THE VERSIONS OF HEALED
ME CAN REPAIR THOSE THROUGH ACTION."

HEART

Anahata

"I AM WORTHY. I AM WORTHY OF LOVE, FORGIVENESS, PEACE AND UNDERSTANDING. I AM WORTHY OF HEALING. I VOW TO MAKE MYSELF MY PRIORITY IN LOVE, GROWTH AND ACTION. IF IT DOES NOT SERVE THE BEST IN ME. IT IS NOT FOR ME."

THROAT

Vissudha

"I CREATE CHANGE. THE WORDS THAT FOLLOW 'I AM' FOLLOW ME. MY WORDS CREATE UNSTOPPABLE, POWERFUL AND POSITIVE ACTION."

THIRD EYE

Ajna

"I SEE BEAUTY IN ALL THINGS. I AM NOT FEARFUL.
I DO NOT LET FEAR BLOCK ME OR SWAY TRUTH. I
SEE THE LESSONS IN MY EXPERIENCES. I AM NOT A
VICTIM. I AM THE MASTER OF MY STORY WRITTEN
WITH GROWTH IN MIND."

CROWN
Sahasrara

"I AM ALL THINGS. AS I MOVE FORWARD, I KNOW, ACCEPT AND UNDERSTAND THAT EVERYTHING IS A REFLECTION OF ME AS WE ARE ALL ONE. I RELEASE ANYTHING THAT NO LONGER SERVES ME OR THE COLLECTIVE IN ASCENSION AND HEALING."

Introducing Crystals and Healing Stones

Crystals, Minerals, Gemstones

Today the common use of the word "crystal" is adopted to cover the many forms of crystals, gemstones, and minerals employed in healing and will be used in this manner in this little guide.

The Origin of Crystals

During history, man has used the power of crystals. Most ancient cultures have held crystals as sacred objects and have used them in ceremony, for meditation, to clarify thoughts, and to heal. Crystals are integrated into our modern technologies, they are used in communications, computers, medical and laser technologies, yet they retain their charm as magical stones. They are naturally shaped by geological procedures and are located worldwide in diverse types of environments. The crystals that we have access to today grew from minerals subjected to strong heat and pressure a million years ago or as a result of sedimentary action over time. Most of the crystals we know about today came from the earth; however, some have arrived here from the heavens or space. These are known as tektites and meteorites.

Types of Crystals

Crystals come in every size, shape, and color. Many are multi-colored. Their mediums follow the modeling of Sacred Geometry. All crystals and gemstones are believed to be living organisms, and they have life energy of their own. They are a valuable part of the Mineral Kingdom, and most are the result of nature, but some are synthetically produced. All different crystals available to us today 'vibrate' on their individual frequency. Numerous crystals are as old as our planet and record their history. Many crystals have a crystalline structure such as clear quartz, while others are in massive form, for instance, the rose quartz. There are numerous crystals found as points, clusters, masses, and stones. They are also tumbled, cut and polished, and formed into shapes such as spheres, eggs, pyramids, wands, obelisks, touchstones etc.

How Do Crystals Work

This might be explained in part through the principle of entrainment and sympathetic resonance: All crystals vibrate on an individual frequency, and we can use this vibration to restore the balance to our bodies as well as our environments, similar to using a tuning fork to match and restore the frequency of a musical note.

Yet another part of the answer is in the creation process. Superheated steam escaping from magma carries minerals that crystallize on the walls of fissures as they cool. All crystals form into an organized pattern, and this structure is why crystals have electrical properties, a fact well known to electronics and computer engineers. The piezoelectric property of a small quartz crystal is what gives your quartz watch its accuracy.

When any crystal is squeezed, it produces an electromagnetic energy field, mostly through the point or a helix. When this pressure is released, it only recharges itself by absorbing free electrons from the atmosphere. This electromagnetic power, or the piezoelectric property, leads to intensifying the aura, or electromagnetic field, giving crystals the ability to help clarify thoughts, channel energy, and heal. Plus, crystals contain minerals with specific healing properties which are reputed to treat or cure specific ailments. You can "tune in" to your crystal and concentrate its power to help achieve your purpose.

A Brief History of Crystals and Healing

It is incredibly accurate to assume that we have had an association with stones and crystals for as long as we have lived. The use of talismans & amulets goes back to the dawn of the human race, but we have no means of confirming how the first of such artifacts were perceived or used. Most early pieces were of organic origin. Beads crafted from mammoth tusks were unearthed from a grave in Sungir, Russia, going back 60,000 years (Upper Palaeolithic period), as well as extant beads made from shell or fossil shark teeth.

Amulets

The earliest amulets are Baltic amber, a few from as early as 30,000 years ago, and amber crystals were found in Britain approximately ten thousand years ago, the end of the last glacial period. The distance they traveled to Britain shows the people of that time their interest. Jet was also common, and jet beads, wrist bands, and necklaces were uncovered in Palaeolithic tombs in Switzerland and Belgium. Xylenol mines have always been in Sinai since 4000 BC. The Christian church in 355 AD forbade Amulettes, but precious stones played a significant role, with Saphir becoming the preferred gem for ecclesiastical rings in the 12th century. Marbodus, Bishop of Rennes in the eleventh century, believed that agate would make the wearer more appealing, convincing, and for God's sake. There were also other symbolic examples, such as the pustule of Christ's death.

Historical References

Ancient Sumerians, who used crystals in magic formulae, made the first historical references on glass use. Ancient Egyptians have used in their jewelry lapis lazuli, turquoise, carnelian, emerald, and transparent quartz. They even graved the same gems with extreme amulets. Stones were used mainly for safety and defense by the pharaohs. Chrysolite was used to combat the night terrors and kill evil spirits (later transcribed as topaz and peridot). Crystals were also aesthetically used by Egyptians. Galena (lead ore) had been ground into a paste, using the so-called kohl-eye shadow.

Similarly, malachite was used. The departed heart was generally identified by green stones, which would be included in the burials. To later Ancient Mexico, green stones were used similarly.

A few of the attributes the ancient Greeks ascribed to crystals, and a number of terms we still use are Greek. The name 'crystal' was derived from the Greek word ice because clear quartz was believed to be water frozen, so sublime that it remained solid. Amethyst means "not intoxicated" and was used as an amulet to discourage drunkenness and hake. The red coloration created when it oxidizes; Hematite comes from a blood term. The iron oxide of Hematite is strongly correlated with ancient Greeks rock, the gods of war Aries. Greek soldiers will rub Hematite before the battle and become purportedly invulnerable over their bodies. Greek sailors wear different amulets even to protect them at sea safely.

In ancient China, Jade was truly valued. Some Chinese writings represent jade beads. Chimes made of garnet and sometimes the Chinese emperors were buried in jade armor about 1000 years ago. Garnet masks are found in Mexico around the same time. In China and South America, Jade was known as a renal healing stone. More recently - 250 years ago - the Maoris of New Zealand had pendants reflecting the ancestors' spirits that were passed by the male line for several generations. The green marble practice continued to this very day parts of New Zealand.

Crystals in Religion

Throughout all religions, crystals and gems played an important role. They are described in the entire Bible, in the Koran, and several other texts. The birthplace is Aaron's breastplate, as stated in the book of Exodus, or 'high priest's breastplate. In the Koran, Carbuncle (garnet) is a fourth heaven. The Kalpa Tree, which is an offering for the gods under Hinduism, is said to have been composed primarily of precious stone and a Buddhist text from the seventh century mentions a diamond throne near the Tree of Knowledge. A million Kalpa Buddhas have sat on this throne. Throughout Jainism, the Kalpa Sutra speaks of Harinegamesi, the supreme leader of the foot troops who has seized and cleaned 14 precious stones and only preserved the most refined essence to assist throughout their transitions.

There is also the Ratnapariksha of Buddhabhatta, an essential ancient lapidary treatise. Some accounts suggest it's Hindu, but most probably, it's Buddhist. The date is uncertain but probably dates back to the sixth century. Diamonds are very much portrayed in this treatise as the king of jewels and are classified by caste. For the Hindu Goddess Indra, the Sanskrit word diamond, vajra, is often synonymous with thunder, and thunder is often related to diamonds. The ruby was respected too. He was an unquenchable fire and was intended to protect the wearer's health and wellbeing. The treatise mentions many other stones and their characteristics.

The Renaissance

Throughout Europe, the qualities of precious and semi-precious stones have been revered in many medical practices since the 11th century during the Renaissance. Stones were usually used in addition to herbal remedies. Hildegard von Binghen and John Mandeville, along with Arnoldus Saxo, were the authors. There are also references to stones with unique strength or defense qualities. In 1232, Hubert de Burgh, presiding justice of Henry III, was suspected of taking a gem from the king's collection, so that the wearing person would be invincible.

Gemstones were often believed to be tainted by Adam's initial sins, to be possessed by angels, or to be treated by a sinner to break from their virtues. Therefore, before you wear, you will be hallowed and sanctified. Today, there is an echo to this idea that crystals are washed and programmed before they are used in crystal cure. While the Renaissance has always embraced the practice of using precious healing stones, the discerning minds of the time wanted to discover how the mechanism worked and to understand it more scientifically.

The Beginning of Crystal Healing

In 1609 Anselmus de Boot, court doctor of Rudolf II of Germany, stated that the existence of good or bad angels was the explanation for every virtue which a gemstone had. The good angels grant gems a special grace, but the poor angels encourage people to believe in the stone alone and not in the gifts given to it by God. He instead calls several stones as beneficial and descends specific attributes to superstitious beliefs. Later that century, in his 'Faithful Lapidary,' Thomas Nichols said gems could not exhibit the effects claimed in the past, as inanimate artifacts. Therefore, the use of significant healing and protective stones started to decline in Europe in the illumination era. A variety of important studies have been done in the earlier half of the 19th century to show the impact of stones on clear-sighted subjects. In one case, the issue believed that the touch of different rocks is not only physical and mental, but also has tastes and smells.

Crystal and Gemstone Meaning

Even though they are no longer used medically, gemstones still have meaning. Mourners widely wore jet until recently, and grenets were used often in times of war. There is a custom in a local family in the southwest of England: each woman's offspring is wearing an antique moon necklace for their marriage, which has been around for centuries. Just a family member recently discovered that this was a sign of fertility.

Until quite recently, if not until now, many tribal communities have continued to use precious stones to heal. New Mexico's Zuni tribe produces fetishes of stone that reflect animal spirits. They were served on polished Turquoise and ground corn consecrated. Wonderful inlaid fantasies are still sold and are rather collectible objects or sculptures, even though they are no longer used much in the spiritual activity. Many native American tribes still hold sacred, particularly turquoise, precious stones. Aborigines and Maoris also have stone and religious activity practices, including some that they share with the world, while other knowledge is still private in their families. It is important to note that, while there is absolutely no overlap between these cultures or the chance of overlap, several examples of gemstones are close to diverse cultures. The ancient civilizations, and even the Aztecs and Mayans, considered Jade a kidney healing stone. Turquoise was worn to offer strength and health worldwide, and jasper almost also provided power and peace.

A New Age Dawns

Throughout the 80s, the use of crystals and gemstones started to reappear as a healing tool with the rise of the New Age movement. Most of the practice came from ancient rituals, with more experimenting and channeling knowledge. The use of crystals was popularized in Katrina Rafael in the '80s, and Melody and Michael Gienger in the '90s.

A substantial percentage of books on the subject are now available, and crystals are also used in magazines and journals. Crystal therapy crosses social and philosophical boundaries. The area of alternative culture is no longer seen as an appropriate, more popular complementary therapy, and many schools now provide it as a subject of qualification.

Different Crystal Shapes

Crystals, especially healing ones, are a great way to boost your energy. Healing crystals have many uses in our day to day life. One of the most well-known and popular benefits for healing crystals is healing the mind and body through meditation. Meditation has long been recognized as a powerful method of healing the mind and soul. Healing crystals are used to focus your attention on areas of the mind that are not connected with physical symptoms or illness.

The healing powers of crystals come from their different shapes and energies. For example, there are healing crystals shaped like hearts, triangles, and spirals. There are also others molded like flowers, angels, and suns. Sometimes, healing crystals are used to connect one's self with spiritual beings or energy. These forces can enhance a person's energy level and bring about an overall sense of calmness and harmony. Crystals can also be used to draw one's energy into the crystal itself, which is called the balancing of yin and yang.

Tumbled Stones

Tumbled stones are a perfect starting point for your crystal journey. The advantages of these pocket-sized crystals are essential for a small sum of money. We also found that several people use a stone rather than the standard energy requirement. Because of its size, rotting stones can be stored in the pocket or purse, placed on the desk inside the car, or under your pillow.

Spheres

Crystal spheres help emit energy in every direction. The perfect symmetry of a field gives the atmosphere harmony, peace, and relaxation energies. Practicing meditation on a globe brings a deep sense of balance, like having the universe in your hand's palm. They integrate your whole being and bind you with your environment's energy.

Pyramids

One of the most efficient tools for the realization and amplification of energy is the pyramid. Several ancient cultures, no one more popular than the ancient Egyptians, have used this sacred tool. They figured pyramids reflect the Sun's rays. Crystals in this spiritual form are meant to use high vibratory energies to increase the strength of manifestation.

Harmonizers

Crystal harmonizers are shaped for mindfulness into cylindrical shapes. Since ancient Romans, these crystal instruments have been designed to cure energy blocks and strength imbalances. Through holding a harmonizer in the left and a harmonizer in the right hand (yin), you revitalize the spiritual energy and maintain a sense of equilibrium.

Cubes

There are several crystals found in the cubic formation. The cube structure is linked to the root chakra. Practicing meditation on cube crystals will help ground your energy and stay connected with the Earth's internal energy. By putting cubic structures in each of the four corners of your house, you will seal, safeguard, and ground your space's energy.

Hearts

Heart-shaped crystals serve to remind you that love is all for you. They are strong allies in helping people to win love and nurture you with inner affection.

Points

Some of the most widely used and useful crystals to work with are crystal points. They are perfect for manifestation, as they help you convey your visions, desires, and aspirations far more easily by transferring your purpose to the world.

Clusters

A crystal cluster tends to occur if several crystal dots grow together on the same matrix. Due to the development of many crystal points, the crystal cluster pulsates at an even higher energy state, directing energy in different directions and working to make it an important crystal.

The Formation of Crystals

What Are Crystals

Crystals are nothing but a group of molecules or atoms. Crystals come in a variety of sizes and shapes, and each one has different characteristics. What they're made from decides how it's going to shape. Few crystals may be formed from salt — these are composed of crystals in a cubed form. Some are extracted from other elements, and they include entirely different shapes. Any examples of such are rubies or gems. Certain factors can produce more than one form. When the carbon dimension is in the shape of a diamond, it could be used to split gemstones, but in many things, we use it every day in specific ways. The most extensive form we use it is supplying our businesses and homes with electricity.

How Are They Formed

A crystal or crystalline solid is a chemical substance whose components are structured in a highly complex microscopic structure, including the atoms, molecules, or ions, developing a crystal lattice that stretches in every direction. Moreover, single macroscopic crystals are typically recognizable by their geometric form, consisting of smooth faces with different character orientations.

A comprehensive research of crystals and their formation is called crystallography. The crystal growth process is called the crystallization or solidification process. The word crystal derives from the ancient Greek term *krustallos*, implying "stone" as well as "rock crystal," from *kruos*, "icy cold, snow."

Most minerals appear as crystals, naturally. Each crystal has an organized, internal atom pattern, with a distinct manner of locking new atoms into that pattern to repeat it repeatedly. The resulting crystal form-such as a cube (like salt) or a six-sided shape (like a snowflake), -mirrors the atoms' internal structure. As crystals expand, they induce interesting differences in temperature and chemical compositions. But students can never find the beautifully formed mineral crystals they display in a museum in their backyard.

That is because the crystals need ideal growing conditions and room to grow to demonstrate their geometrical shapes and flat surfaces readily. When they grow close to each other, many unique crystals mesh together to create a conglomerated mass. It's is the case with most rocks, such as granite, which consists of many small mineral crystals described above. The museum-quality samples seen in the images here developed in spacious environments that allowed unrestrained formation of the geometric forms.

The internal structure of atoms influences the physicochemical properties of all minerals and colors. Light combines with multiple particles to create different colors. Many minerals in their pure state are colorless; even so, atomic structure impurities induce color. For example, quartz is usually colorless, but appears in various colors from fuchsia to brown to deep amethyst purple, depending on the number and form of contaminants in its composition. Quartz represents ice in its colorless nature. The origin for crystal originally derives from the Greek term krystallos-ice-because the ancient Greeks claimed that pure quartz was solid ice so strong it couldn't melt away.

Scientists usually call crystals "rising," even though they are not alive. They branch and bristle in subterranean gardens, as billions and billions of atoms connect in repeating three dimensions. Each crystal begins to grow larger as more particles are added. Many produce rich in mineral salts from water, but they also grow from pulverized rock and even vapor. Atoms join in an impressive variety of crystal forms, under the influence of different pressures and temperatures. This diversity and beauty of shape and symmetry that the research of minerals has long attracted scientists to it.

Symmetry is a standard sequence of component pieces, repeatedly. Balance is found in nature-a butterfly's paired wings, the whorls and petals in a sunflower, a snowflake pattern, a spider's legs, and minerals are no different. These repetitive patterns exist in crystals within the simple atomic structure and represent crystal faces' design.

You will always see a mineral crystal's signature symmetry from the human eye, but you can need to look at it with a mirror or microscope if the crystal is thin. At first, it can be challenging to identify geometric shapes in crystals, but practice helps: the more examples you look at, the more symmetry and crystals you can notice. Some spec-dimensions, however, do not have excellently-formed crystals and are hard to characterize even for experts.

Crystal Structure

The scientific definition of a "crystal" is based on the microstructure arrangement of the atoms within it, called the structure of crystals. A crystal is a solid in which the atoms form a regular arrangement. Not all the crystals are solids. For example, as liquid water starts to freeze, the transition of process occurs with tiny ice crystals rising until they merge, creating a polycrystalline structure. Growing of the small crystals (called "crystallites" or "grains") in the final block of ice is a true crystal with a regular arrangement of the atoms.

But the entire polycrystal has no recurrent arrangement of atoms, as its periodic sequence at the boundaries of the grain is broken. Most synthetic macroscopic solids are polycrystalline, like almost all the metals, ceramics, sand, stone, etc. Solids, which are neither crystalline nor polycrystalline, such as glass, are known as amorphous solids, also termed glassy, vitreous, or non-crystalline. These do not have a periodic, even microscopic order. There are significant distinctions between crystalline solids and amorphous materials: the process of creating a glass, most importantly, does not unleash the residual heat of fusion, but instead forms a crystal.

A crystal structure (a structure of atoms in a crystal) is defined by its unit cell, a small theoretical box in a particular geographical arrangement that contains one or more particles. To form the crystal, the unit cells are stacked in tri-dimensional space. A crystal's consistency is limited by the fact that the unit cells stack evenly, without any holes. There are 219 potential symmetries of crystals, called crystallographic groupings of space. These are classified into seven crystal systems, including the cubic crystal system.

What Unique Properties Do Crystals Have?

Crystals can have elements called flat surfaces. They may develop geometric forms like triangles, rectangles, and squares. The shapes derive directly from the combination of molecules or atoms that make up the crystal. Smaller and bigger crystals formed from the same molecules should have similar profiles in the very same method. Seven different types of crystal, also named lattices, exist. And are Cubic, Trigonal, Triclinic, Hexagonal, Orthorhombic, Tetragonal, and Monoclinic.

Crystal Collection

Whenever you want to buy something, it is better to have thorough knowledge about it before making a buying decision. The same is true when you plan to buy a crystal for yourself. Prior research helps you open your mind about a particular thing. It makes your buying process easy and adds value to it. To make things easy for you, in this chapter, I am describing the qualities of a few popular crystals.

1. Amethyst

This beautiful purple crystal has a soothing and relaxing vibe about it. It is one of those excellent crystals that you can use during meditation. Its powerful rays help you connect with your inner self. If you're new to spirituality, it's an excellent crystal to get started with.

The amethyst crystal can be specifically beneficial for people with the following zodiac signs:

Pisces, Virgo, Aquarius, and Capricorn.

2. Desert Rose Selenite

Desert rose selenite is a beautiful stone that looks like a rose. Its color ranges from white and cream to brown. It is also commonly known as sand rose, selenite rose, desert rose rock, gypsum desert rose, gypsum rose, and gypsum rosettes.

Desert Rose Selenite consists of calming and rejuvenating energy to relieve stress while boosting your willpower. When you meditate, holding a desert rose in your hand, it brings clarity of the mind and cleanses your body of all negative energies.

The Desert Rose Crystal is especially beneficial for people having the zodiac signs Taurus.

3. Rose Quartz

This crystal is also referred to as the 'love crystal'. This stone is available in a variety of pink colors. Rose quartz is commonly used for attracting and keeping love, as well as protecting relationships. The Rose Quartz can also help to heal your heart from disappointment and pain.

People having the zodiac signs Libra and Taurus can significantly benefit from this crystal.

4. Hematite

Hematite is often recommended to use to ground and balance you in your life. Its color ranges include red to brown and black to grey to silver. If you are under stress and need to feel calm and centered, Hematite can be a perfect choice for you. This crystal can also help to banish any negative feelings which result from stress or anxiety.

The hematite crystal can be fantastic for people with zodiac signs Aries and Aquarius.

5. Iron Pyrite

The Iron Pyrite is a beautiful crystal with a metallic shine. It's available in pale brass-yellow color. It is widely used to disperse any negative energy or any physical danger. This can also help magnify your intellectual skills and memory.

The Iron Pyrite Crystal is specifically recommended for people with the zodiac signs Leo.

6. Tiger Eye

This crystal is usually amber to brown. It is thought to be beneficial for maintaining and growing wealth. The Tiger Eye is also known to help create understanding and awareness. It can also be a great stone to calm your nerves when you are feeling stressed

The Tiger Eye Crystal can be especially beneficial for Capricorns.

7. Raw Emerald

The eye-catching vivid green crystal is often called the stone for 'successful love'. This crystal can promote focus, clear negativity and encourage loyalty and sensitivity. It creates intense energy in your life that can be very useful to strengthen your relationship.

The Raw Emerald Crystal is amazing for people with the following zodiac signs Taurus, Gemini, and Aries.

8. Citrine

This sparkly yellow to brownish orange crystal is often used because of its warm and optimistic energy. This is one of those few

stones that don't require to be cleansed or recharged. This crystal also helps to fend off any negative energy that comes your way.

The Citrine Crystal can be specifically recommended for people with the following zodiac signs:

Gemini, Aries, Libra, and Leo.

9. Celestine

The Celestine crystal is mostly colorless, but it is also available in red, milky white, yellow, orange, and blue colors. Blue is its most expensive variety. This crystal is excellent for calming and balancing. It is also thought to help people remember their dreams. Celestine can also help provide clarity and peace to your body.

The Celestine Crystal is quite beneficial for Geminis.

10. Clear Quartz

Quartz crystal is a pure and powerful energy source. This crystal is colorless and transparent. It is also known as "the master healer." This crystal is ideal for people trying to get a better perspective and richer understanding. This crystal promotes self-awareness and stimulates your brain. This crystal could be a great stone to use if you are feeling tired, both mentally and physically.

The Clear Quartz Crystal is equally beneficial for all zodiac signs.

How to Select Your Crystal and Care for It

Select the Best Crystal

Now that you know a lot about chakra and how healing crystals can help you balance them, the next step is to select a crystal for you. Whether you want a crystal to balance a specific chakra or get stones for all seven chakras, the choices are unlimited. Several stones are suitable for each chakra. Some stones may have a more significant impact on your than others have. So, the question is how to know which one is best for you? Well, there is no standard rule for it. However, with some research and practice, you can certainly pick the best stone for you. Let's suppose; you want to balance your root chakra. After reading this book, you know that red jasper, garnet, and bloodstone can help you achieve your purpose. So, one ideal way is to buy three to four appropriate stones and see which one works best for you. However, choosing this method will be very costly. So below are some other ways that can be beneficial for you.

Ask the Universe to Help You

A lot of people benefit from this method. They ask the universe to help them choose the right stone for them. Sounds weird? Well, it may seem strange to you at the moment. However, when you enter the world of mindfulness and spirituality, this will make sense to you. When you ask the divine power for the crystal that will work for your highest good, you will answer. Be open and receptive to whatever crystal comes your way first. If you are still doubtful about this method, give it a try, and you will be amazed to see the results.

Use Your Intuition

This method has always worked for me. It is often said that you don't choose the crystal, the crystal chooses you. So, what are you waiting for? Visit your nearby shop to let your right crystal find you. Now the question is how to use your intuition. Now let's suppose you want to buy a crystal to balance your throat chakra. You know that all the crystals with subtle blue color such as aquamarine and turquoise are good for it. But you want to buy any one of them. When you visit the gemstone shop, walk over to the area where there are blue stones. Close your eyes and run your hands over each stone. You can even hold each stone in your hand and squeeze it. Don't be judgmental or get into a pre-convinced notion. Just focus on your manifestation and your physical and emotional sensations. Observe how you feel. Do you feel a soothing heat in your palms? Do you feel some energy charging you? Or do you feel tranquil?

Repeat this step with each crystal and pick the one that gave you the most fantastic feeling. Moreover, also notice that when you look at the crystals, which crystal attracts you the most in terms of shape, color, and energy. Believe it or not, the stone which is right for you will draw you towards itself with magnetic energy.

Choose the Crystal According to Your Birth Month

This is another effective way. Once you are sure about the chakra you want to balance, search for the stone which is best for you according to your birth month and zodiac sign. You can research it on your own, or you can consult a crystal healer to help you with your selection.

Experiment with Different Crystals

This is an excellent method if you want to develop a deep insight about crystals and their healing properties. However, this is a time-consuming method, and you can take advantage of it by observing each crystal's power. Moreover, it is an expensive choice as well. If you are a beginner in the world of crystals and stones, I would recommend you choose from the first three methods.

Care for Your Crystal

It is indeed an excellent decision to buy a crystal to soothe your body, mind, and soul. However, if you want to get the maximum benefits from their energy, you must care for them and cleanse them from time to time. Crystals are potent sources of energy. They often absorb some forces from the environment that may be misaligned with yours. Even when you buy a crystal, it has already traveled long distances from the source to different sellers. Therefore, it is necessary to cleanse and recharge your crystals to restore them to their natural state.

The following are some of the methods that you can adopt to cleanse your crystals.

Water

Water is the easiest and most handy way to cleanse your stones. Water is beneficial to neutralize all the negative energy stored inside your stone. Just keep your stone under the running water or a faucet and wash it religiously for a minute. Could you not rub it too hard? Let the water do its work. Pat dry it when you are done. Avoid using this method for soft or fragile stones.

Salt Water

Salt is a powerful mineral that can absorb unwanted and harmful energy. If possible, collect a bowl of fresh seawater and soak your stones in it. However, if seawater is not available, you can mix plain water and table salt into a container and soak your stones in it. It will remove all the negative energy from your crystals. Let your stones soak for a few hours. This method is also suitable for hard stones. Avoid using it for stones that are soft, porous, or contain trace metals, such as malachite, selenite, halite, calcite, lepidolite, and Angelite.

Natural Light

What could be the most significant source of energy than natural light? The sun's powerful rays and the moon's soft power are the two great ways to cleanse and recharge your stones. Set your stone out before nightfall and bring it in before 11 am the next day. This will let your stone bathe in the light of both the moon and sun. Don't expose your crystals in the sunlight for so long. It will weather the crystal's surface. Avoid using exposing vibrant stones such as amethyst and soft rocks such as celestite, halite, and selenite in the sun.

Sage

Sage is a sacred herb that contains a myriad of healing benefits. Burning sage leaves in the home to eliminate any harmful energies is a popular traditional way. It serves the same purpose for your stone as well. Take a handful of sage, keep it in a bowl, and burn it. Now move the stone through the smoke emitting from the bowl. Allow the smoke to envelop the stone for about 30 seconds. This is the best cleaning method, and it is equally great for all types of stones.

Use Other Stones

Crystals like carnelian and clear quartz are associated with purification. They are considered to be very useful to cleanse other crystals. Stack these stones on top of any crystals that need clearing, or keep them all in the same bag when you travel.

Why Do Chakras Need Healing

Everything in our universe radiates energy, from the most massive mountain or sea, to the smallest blade of grass, to every single cell in the human body. All of our cells emit different amounts of energy, and other cells emit various types of energy depending on when they're in the body and what their function is. Due to the special nature of the body's energy, there are several multiple sockets located at critical points of the body through which this energy can circulate in and out of a continuous flow. They are known as the chakras.

The word chakra means "wheel" in Sanskrit, although it's not like every other wheels we have ever seen. Chakra energy spins outwards as it moves our body's force out and into the field around us, and rotates clockwise to pull the power out of our outer world into our body. It is the intensity state of our chakras that ultimately determines the direction in which our energy will flow, either by drawing power into our body or by releasing it outward. But are our Chakras physical entities? Are the actual little wheels spinning in the seven main centers of our body? No, no. They're not made up of matter; they are energetic. But like a fan's whirling blades, only because you cannot see them, it does not mean they are not there.

You might be beginning to wonder how we can know that there are chakras if we can't physically see them. It's a legitimate point, and one for which science has not yet discovered a concrete answer. It has been studied and demonstrated time and time again during the Ayurvedic and Yogic traditions and in the Chinese concepts of qi and meridians. The influence of our body's energy, the life force that circulates through us, and the quantum field's strength are things that our scholarly abilities have yet to catch up with.

Our chakras exist at seven points along our body, each correlated with a separate set of organs. It should not be too shocking that our chakras' areas directly relate to our body places where the essential systems use a great deal of energy. For example, the one between the eyes sits around our visual center, of course, and our brain's prefrontal cortex. This location is the epicenter of our decision-making, planning, and alignment. There is far too much energy needed in that part of our body that it tends to make total sense to have an energy outlet located in a convenient location. Chakras can either be open or closed, hyperactive, or underactive, depending on how they can flow through them. And that flow is influenced by the open or constrained state of your body as well as energy body.

Chakras and Your Energetic Frequency

The energy from our chakras affects our physical processes through inhibition and relaxation. Note that chakras are like wheels whose function is to keep power going and narrow or close down to protect against negative energy. To account for a small, subactive chakra, another chakra may become overactive, transmitting your low-frequency vibrations more quickly and requires more balance in the chakra healing cycle. That, in effect, generates a lower frequencies reality and extends it. If your chakras are energy centers that emit, absorb, are they the origins of, or are they the product of your frequency?? Are chickens or eggs your chakras?

The double role of the chakras is in the relation between mind and body regarding your consciousness and physical self. When you focus on your body, your mind is on the way, and vice versa. The same goes for your chakra frequency and strength. If you are in the ego phase, it influences the energy flow inside your chakras and the entire physical as well as energy system producing, among other things, more energy needs of the body and chakra.

Only note, if you operate at a lower frequency, then 1) your perception is created, as your five senses pick up what you apply the mind to (This is where we are, all things reinforcing it) and 2) your resonating frequency is what you put in the quantum field and what you pulled into yourself by your chakras, which impacts you.

Balance Is Key in Chakra Healing

No one chakra is stronger or more relevant than others in the energy body balance and chakra healing cycle. You don't want extra energy from the heart chakra and less power from the throat chakra; it does not work that way. Ideally, all seven chakras are cured, equilibrated, opened, and hummed so that energy flows into and out of your body. The remarkable fact is that your body will find a way to transfer energy into it and out (unless you suggest that your ego will stick to it, of course). If one of your chakras is inactive or not, there was an outstanding possibility that another chakra is hyperactive. Since your body needs to maintain energy balance in your chakras, going in either direction (underactive or overactive) in one chakra can have adverse effects and detrimental effects on the energy body and the chakra healing process. The underactive chakra sends another chakra into an overdrive that draws extra energy away from the body. The following examples illustrate how you can behave or feel when your chakras are robbed of harmony and need healing. The first list lists the structural elements connected to each chakra and the possible physical signs that might tell you anything is out of the question.

ROOT CHAKRA TRAUMA

Can leave you feeling unsafe. Nervous. Disconnected from Earth and, therefore, your body. "Up in the clouds." Distracted. But it can also make you feel like nothing ever "takes off." Your great ideas never land or become a reality; you plan but never implement.

SACRAL CHAKRA TRAUMA

Can have you feeling shameful of your body. Disconnected to your sexuality. Dry. Not interested in sex. Lacking creativity. Feeling unnurturing and unable to perform. It can also block affection, abundance, positive energy.

SOLAR PLEXUS TRAUMA

Can have you over indulging in food, drinks, drugs, people, toxic relationships. But it can also have you hiding your true self. Feeling like no one will ever truly understand you or see the real you. You may feel like you need to 'perform' to please others and be accepted. You may base your worth on what you can sacrifice for others and be a people pleaser. Someone who would do anything for acknowledgment or praise.

HEART CHAKRA TRAUMA

Can have you rejecting love and relationships, but it will also have you hating yourself and sabotaging any chance you have at happiness. One may feel heavy; it may be hard to breathe. One may also carry heavy grief and weight from grudges.

THROAT CHAKRA TRAUMA

May make it hard for you to communicate and express yourself. But it may also have you replaying toxic words, self-destructive memories, abusive attacks from others OVER AND OVER again.

THIRD EYE TRAUMA

Can make it hard to see others' perspectives and truths. People can become rigid in their thinking. It can also take dreams, cause headaches, memory block, limitation to psychic gifts, and make it harder to learn.

CROWN CHAKRA TRAUMA

Can make it hard to have faith. Hard to believe in the goodness of humanity and feel one with others in a deeper soul level connection. It can also drain you spiritually and create confusion.

How Can You Balance Chakras with Crystals?

Many times, we feel upset and distressed for no apparent reason. Even after having all the luxuries and comforts of life, we can't feel happiness. We think something is wrong, but we don't seem to figure out what. We often brush such feelings aside, assuming that we are overthinking. However, it may not just be overthinking. You may be going through such emotions because your chakras are imbalanced. By balancing your chakras, you will feel a dramatic change in your feelings and emotions. Balanced and aligned chakras are essential for your health and life. Even people who don't believe in spiritual practices and treatments can benefit from having their chakras balanced. There are several methods to balance your chakras; one of the most effective is balancing chakras using crystals. It is mainly because of the colors and energy order chakras.

Similarly, the energy emerging from a crystal is often guided by its color. Therefore, using crystals to align chakras is very helpful. As discussed in previous chapters, each chakra is linked with different parts, organs, and muscles. A blockage or imbalance in chakras can cause physical and emotional discomfort in its associated regions. There are four ways crystals can be used to put chakras in order.

1. Place chakra crystals on your body according to their respective chakras.
2. Keep chakra crystals near you while resting.
3. Meditate with chakra crystals.
4. Wear crystals.

Before diving into the details of these methods, let's first understand which crystal is best suited to each chakra.

Red Root Chakra

For red rootchakra, red or black stones such as red jasper, bloodstone or garnet are suitable.

Orange Pelvic Charka

Carnelian or citrine is the best crystal to balance the pelvic chakra.

Yellow Solar Plexus Chakra

To balance this chakra, the recommended crystals are golden topaz, tiger's eye and amber

Green Heart Chakra

Rose quartz, green jasper, emerald and green aventurine can help you balance the heart chakra.

Blue Throat Chakra

Light blue stones like turquoise and aquamarine can be beneficial to balance this chakra.

Indigo Third Eye Chakra

This chakra can be balanced using lapislazuli, sodalite and amethyst.

Violet Crown Chakra

Clear quartz, selenite, amethyst and diamond can be used to stimulate this chakra.

Now that we know about the crystals that can be helpful to balance the seven chakras let's discuss how you can benefit from these crystals.

Place Chakra Crystals on Your Body According to Their Respective Chakras

This is one of the best ways to balance your chakras. In this method, you place chakra crystals directly on your body in line with the chakras. When the healing energy emitting from the stones enters your body, your chakras get stimulated and balanced. To do this, choose a quiet and peaceful place where there is no distraction. Then lie down on a comfortable flat surface. Keep chakra crystals with you and start with the root chakra.

1. Place red crystal of root chakra at the base of your spine.

2. Place orange stone of pelvic chakra a couple of inches below the navel.

3. Place yellow stone of solar plexus chakra exactly on the navel.

4. Place a green stone of heart chakra in the center of your chest.

5. Place blue stone of throat chakra on your throat.

6. Place indigo stone of third eye chakra between your eyebrows.

7. Place violet crystal of crown chakra above your head. If the crystal is pointed, place it with the point directing up.

Now close your eyes and let your body absorb the healing energy. Keep your body and nerves relaxed. Imagine that the colorful rays of stones are entering your body and reaching every cell. The healing power is erasing all the negativity from your body. If you want, you can also play soothing piano music in the background. (do it before you lie down and keep the volume slow so that you don't get distracted). Enjoy the tranquillity and focus as long as you want. Each crystal has a particular frequency and energy. When this frequency is aligned with your body, it creates a connection between your mind and body. This connection strengthens your focus and balances your chakras.

Keep Chakra Crystals Near You While Resting

Keep all seven chakra stones under your pillow at night or whenever you are sleeping. Moreover, you can keep them near you while resting or reading a book. The energy of these stones is potent. It will keep impacting your mind and body. The healing power of these stones works like a magnet. As it reaches your body, it attracts the chakras, and hence they get balanced.

Meditate with Chakra Crystals

Meditation is an excellent way of improving your focus and mindfulness. When it is combined with chakra stones, its benefit is enhanced. Just hold chakra stones in your hands while meditating. Envision that the colorful energy of these stones is healing your body and mind. If you are experiencing a particular problem due to your chakras' blockage, or if you have a specific aim related to that problem in your mind, imagine that it is being resolved as you absorb the power of these stones. Remember that results cannot be achieved overnight. You have to be persistent and regular in your practice. With consistency, you will experience the amazing benefits of this method.

Wear Crystals

This is one of the easiest ways. Due to our busy schedule, we often don't get time to meditate or place chakra stones on our bodies. However, we can still benefit from the power of these stones. Keep these stones close to your body, such as keeping them in your pocket or wearing them as jewelry. The longer you keep them with you, the more their frequencies will do their work to heal your chakras.

Balancing your chakras will help you become focused and mindful. It can help you understand your inner self. When you are more self-aware, you can find ways to bring peace and happiness in your life. Using chakra stones to balance your chakras can help heal them and bring stability, positivity, calmness, and health to your life.

Chakra Crystal Healing Tips

Functions of Crown Chakra

Crown chakra is the seventh chakra located at the top of your head. This is why it is named crown. This chakra significantly impacts your central nervous system, muscular system, and skin. It serves as the entry point for all sources of energy. It then distributes that energy throughout your body and all other chakras. On an emotional level, crown chakra plays a huge role in connecting you to the universe and the divine source of creation. It gives you an awareness of your highest spiritual self. It makes you realize that everything in this world is interconnected and everything is governed by divine power. When your crown chakra is aligned correctly, you enjoy the sense of gratitude, trust and faith.

Imbalance in Crown Chakra

When your crown chakra is blocked, you feel anxious, distressed, and fearful because your connection with your highest spiritual self is lost. The outlook of your thoughts becomes limited because you are unable to sense divine plans.

Healing Crystals

Two of the best healing stones for balancing crown chakra are clear quartz and amethyst. Clear quartz is also known as the "Master Healer." Its powerful energy helps you achieve spiritual and mental clarity. Amethyst is another strong crystal. Its purple, vibrant energy helps you balance emotions, alleviates stress, and calms extreme feelings like anger, negativity, and anxiety.

Functions of Third Eye Chakra

The third eye chakra is the sixth chakra, located between the eyebrows. This chakra is associated with intuition, wisdom, and sixth sense. It´s the inner eye that gives us insight into our inner self and capabilities. The third eye chakra correlates to our mental abilities, psychological skills, and how we evaluate beliefs and attitudes. This powerful chakra helps us acknowledge the truth and control our minds. When this chakra is aligned, we are focused and can enjoy the benefits of mindfulness.

Imbalance in Third Eye Chakra

A dis-harmony in this chakra impacts your psychological mind state. You experience frequent mood swings and anxiety. In physical terms, people with an imbalance in third eyes chakra often have headaches, blurred vision, and sinus problems.

Healing Crystals

The best healing crystals for this chakra are amethyst and lapis lazuli. Amethyst is also known as the stone of "Total Awareness." It will bring you a perspective that is omnipotent and multidimensional.' Sodalite is a powerful stone to heal your third eye chakra. It comes in different colors, but it is well known for its blue variety. The cool blue rays of sodalite are beneficial to enhance focus and memory. Wearing this crystal also alleviates distracting thoughts and stimulates intelligence. The calming energy of sodalite soothes fears and connects you to your higher self.

Functions of Throat Chakra

The throat chakra is the fifth chakra, and it is located at the centre of the neck at throat level. This chakra serves as the passage of energy between the head and lower parts of the body. The throat chakra relates to communication and your ability to express your feelings and thoughts.

Imbalance in Throat Chakra

An imbalance in this chakra often leads to trouble in communication ability. Some people develop excessive fear of speaking in front of others; while others talk too much or inappropriately. A blockage in this chakra often leads a person to become introvert. They lose connection with their purpose in life.

Healing Crystal

The two best stones to balance throat chakra are turquoise and aquamarine. The ocean blue color of turquoise eliminates negativity and restores confidence to speak and express your thoughts effectively. Another recommended stone to balance throat chakra, aquamarine, is used to cleanse and stimulate your mind and soul. It enhances courage and promotes tolerance and compassion while dissipating fear.

Functions of Heart Chakra

The heart chakra is the fourth chakra located in the center of your chest. This chakra is associated with maintaining relationships, love for oneself and others. It stimulates compassion, empathy, forgiveness, and acceptance. When this chakra is open, you feel content and grateful for all the beauty around you.

Imbalance in Heart Chakra

A dis-harmony in this chakra often results in difficulty in dealing with others. People become closed down and feel jealous of other people's blessings and abilities. They find it hard to forgive others and hold grudges that eventually cost them their peace. Some people also develop codependency. They go out of their way to please people around them and seek their approval. This leads to insecurities and self-sabotaging thoughts.

Healing Crystal

The best healing stones for this chakra are green aventurine and emerald. Emerald is considered as the purest form of green-ray energy. It is also called the stone of "successful love." It can help you bring balance to relationships, encourage loyalty, and enhance unconditional love. Another best stone to align your heart chakra is green aventurine. Its soft energy is excellent for promoting harmony. It is amazing to balance friction or negativity in a relationship while releasing unhealthy patterns and bringing new opportunities.

Functions of Solar Plexus Chakra

Solar plexus chakra is the third chakra located at the upper part of your navel. This chakra is associated with willpower, self-control, and mental abilities. When this chakra is aligned, you feel confident and optimistic about your responsibilities. The energy of this chakra allows you to transform lethargy into action and movement. It will enable you to meet challenges and move forward in your life.

Imbalance in Solar Plexus Chakra

When your solar plexus chakra is blocked, the feelings of helplessness and irresponsibility take a toll on you. You may feel self-pity and often blame others for your problems. In some cases, people become controlling and authoritative over people related to them. Their thoughts are not aligned. They lack clear direction and purpose.

Healing Crystal

The two most recommended stones to balance solar plexus chakra are golden topaz and amber. Golden topaz is a protective stone against all kinds of negativity. It eases fear, anger, and depression. Golden topaz prevents sleepwalking and nightmare while bringing joy, health, motivation, and a sense of forgiveness. Amber is another powerful stone to heal your solar plexus chakra. It promotes healing and renews the nervous system. It absorbs pain and negative energy, helping to alleviate stress. Amber soothes depression, enhances intellectual capabilities, and promotes self-confidence and creative self-expression.

Functions of Sacral Chakra

The sacral chakra is the second chakra located about two to three inches below the navel. The sacral chakra is associated with the expressions of emotions and sexual pleasure. When your sacral chakra is open, you feel motivated and enjoy the bounties of life. This chakra plays a significant role in developing flexibility in our life.

Imbalance in Sacral Chakra

When this chakra is blocked, your emotions get out of your control. Their feelings rule some people, while others feel out of touch with themselves. Some people develop sexual obsessions, while others experience a lack of sexual desire or satisfaction. In short, a dis-harmony in sacral chakra adversely affects your mood and mental state, and you feel agitated and miserable no matter what the situation is.

Healing Crystal

The best crystal to heal sacral chakra is orange carnelian. It has the sunset color, which is very useful to soothe your mind and body. This powerful stone can calm your emotions and boost your intuition, passion, and self-belief. It will also balance the flowing energy while encouraging confidence.

Functions of Root Chakra

The root chakra is the first chakra located at the base of the spine. This chakra is associated with the feeling of safety, security, and survival. It is about your basic survival needs such as food, shelter, safety, and your emotional needs, such as feeling safe and grounded. When your root chakra is open, you feel healthy and emotionally stable.

Imbalance in Root Chakra

When your root chakra is out of balance, you get caught up in your emotions. It leads to excessive negativity and insecurities.

Many times, people with imbalanced root chakra develop greed and avarice. Some people may experience eating disorders. Blocked root chakra often makes you feel threatened, anxious, and panicked. Physical issues potentially caused by a blocked Root Chakra include a sore lower back, low energy levels, and cold extremities.

Healing Crystals

Two of the best stones to balance your root chakra are bloodstone and red jasper. Bloodstone is a powerful cleanser and healer that strongly connects with the Root Chakra. It comes in a combination of green and red colors. The powerful energy emitting from these colors represents a blend of growth, fearlessness, and strength. Using this crystal blocks negativity and protects against threats. Similarly, with its spiritually grounding energy, red jasper ensures you remain 'connected' with your real power. It will help your meditation and other spiritual practices.

HEALING MANTRA CODES

CROWN
Sahasrara

I AM ALL

THIRD EYE
Ajna

I SEE BEAUTY IN ALL

THROAT
Vissudha

I CREATE MY REALITY

HEART
Anahata

I AM WORTHY

SOLAR PLEXUS
Manipura

I AM IN CHARGE

SACRAL
Svadhisthana

I AM FREE

ROOT
Muladhara

I AM SAFE

Conclusion

"You have the power to heal your life, and you need to know that. We think so often that we are helpless, but we're not. We always have the power of our minds...Claim and consciously use your power."

— Louise L. Hay

Congratulations!

You have reached the first milestone in your journey to chakra healing, i.e., gaining knowledge about how chakras work and can be unblocked and healed. Reading about chakras is an excellent first step. It shows you are determined to bring a positive change in your life. However, any information is only useful when it is practically applied in our lives. So, the next step for you is to start implementing the techniques presented in this book to heal your chakras. Shifting your focus and awareness on healing your energy centers can boost your overall well-being. But remember that chakra healing is a form of alternative medicine, and every alternative medicine requires time and dedication to show its effects. Therefore, be patient and persistent, and you will experience the fantastic benefits of chakra healing on your physical and mental health.

One of the most special blessings in this world is good health — physical, mental, and emotional, and the purpose of writing this book was to promote a healthier and more active lifestyle. Being busy fulfilling our lives' duties and responsibilities, our bodies and minds get cluttered with harmful toxins and damaging thoughts. We don't realize, but with each passing day, these all elements affect our lives adversely. Slowly and gradually, anxiety, stress, worries, and depressing thoughts take a toll on our lives. Besides, we also develop several physical health issues. To put it simple, our lives become messed up, and we can't seem to figure out what is wrong with us. Luckily, you are one of those fortunate people who are mindful of the significance of physical, mental, and emotional health. Therefore, you chose to read this book. Developing mindfulness is the key to transform our lives.

Investing some time dedicatedly to chakra balance through crystal healing, meditation, yoga, praying, and affirmations can do wonders to your life. Moreover, by becoming aware of these invisible chakras—and signs of an imbalance—you can try out new self-help methods other than the ones described in this book to tackle your emotional and physical problems. When your chakras are balanced, you will find that your life opens up to new horizons very easily and quickly. It's time to explore your chakras and balance them to enjoy a better and healthier life.

Also available from Jay K. Morley:

Chakra Opening: The Ultimate Guide to Awaken the Power Within, Balance Chakras, and Heal Your Mind and Body

The Book Of Chakras: The Complete Guide To Awaken, Open And Balance The Chakras For Complete Self-Healing With Meditation And Stones